Pluto in a Tutu

By Carmel Reilly

Ruby wants to win
the pet photo contest.

She can win a trip!

Ruby looked at a big map with Dad.

"I want to win so much!" she said.

"Why?" said Dad.

"I want to see some deer.
And cats that wave!" said Ruby.
"And eat lots of sushi!"

"I might see Fuji!" said Ruby.

"Yes, Fuji is a very high hill," said Dad.

"What will you do to win?"
said Dad.

"My photo must truly stand out,"
said Ruby.

"Oh!" yelled Ruby.
"I will get Pluto to jump into my hula hoop!"

Pluto smiled.

He did not get it.

Ruby trained Pluto.

First, she put a tutu on him.

"Come on, Pluto!" said Ruby.
"You can do it!"

But Pluto could not jump that high.

They trained for weeks.

Pluto could not do it.

One day, Ruby came up
with a plan.

"This will help you jump high,
Pluto," she said.

Ruby put Pluto up on a box.

Ruby held up her hula hoop,
and Pluto jumped ...

Ruby's photo was the best!

She could go on the trip!

Pluto in a tutu jumps into a hula hoop.

1st

CHECKING FOR MEANING

1. Why did Ruby want to go on the trip? *(Literal)*

2. What did Ruby want to teach Pluto to do? *(Literal)*

3. What else could Ruby have done to help Pluto jump through the hula hoop? *(Inferential)*

EXTENDING VOCABULARY

sushi	What is *sushi*? What do you do with sushi? What ingredients are in sushi?
hula hoop	What is a *hula hoop*? How do you play with a hula hoop?
tutu	What is a *tutu*? Who usually wears a tutu? What other special clothing do dancers wear? E.g. dancing shoes, stockings, ballet dress.

MOVING BEYOND THE TEXT

1. Have you ever tried to teach a trick to your pet? What was the trick? Were you successful?

2. What are some special tricks animals can do? Which animals are easiest to teach? Can all animals do tricks?

3. Have you ever been in a competition to win a special prize? What was the prize? What did you have to do to win the prize?

4. Which animals sometimes wear clothes? Why do pet owners put clothes on their animals? What do they wear?

SPEED SOUNDS

oo	ue	ew	ui	u_e

ou	u	oe	o

PRACTICE WORDS

Ruby

to

sushi

Fuji

you

truly

do

Pluto

hoop

You

tutu

hula